Eleven Motets

Recent Researches in the Music of the Renaissance is one of four quarterly series (Middle Ages and Early Renaissance, Renaissance, Baroque Era, Classical Era) which make public the early music that is being brought to light in the course of current independent musicological research.

Each volume is devoted to works by a single composer or in a single genre of composition, chosen because of their potential interest to scholars and performers, and prepared for the press according to the standards that govern the preparation of all reliable historical editions.

Whenever the demand for works in the series is great enough to warrant the expense, reprints are published for the benefit of performers.

Correspondence should be addressed:

A-R Editions, Inc.
53 Livingston Street
New Haven, Connecticut 06511

Philippe Rogier

1368

Eleven Motets

**RECENT RESEARCHES IN THE MUSIC OF
THE RENAISSANCE • VOLUME II**

Edited by Lavern J. Wagner

1966
A-R Editions, Inc.
New Haven

Contents

CANTVS,
PHILIPPI ROGERII,
MI
INVICTISS. PHILIPPI II.
HISPANIARVM REGIS, ETC.
CHORI MVSICI PRÆFECTI.
SACRARVM MODVLATIONVM, QVAS VVLGO
Motecta appellant: quæ Quaternis, Quinis, Senis, &
octonis vocibus concinuntur.
LIBER PRIMVS.

NEAPOLI, Ex Typogr. Stelliolæ, ad Portam Regalem.

Plate I. *Cantus, Philippi Rogerii, . . . sacrarum modulationum,
quas vulgo Motecta appellant . . .* (1595): title page

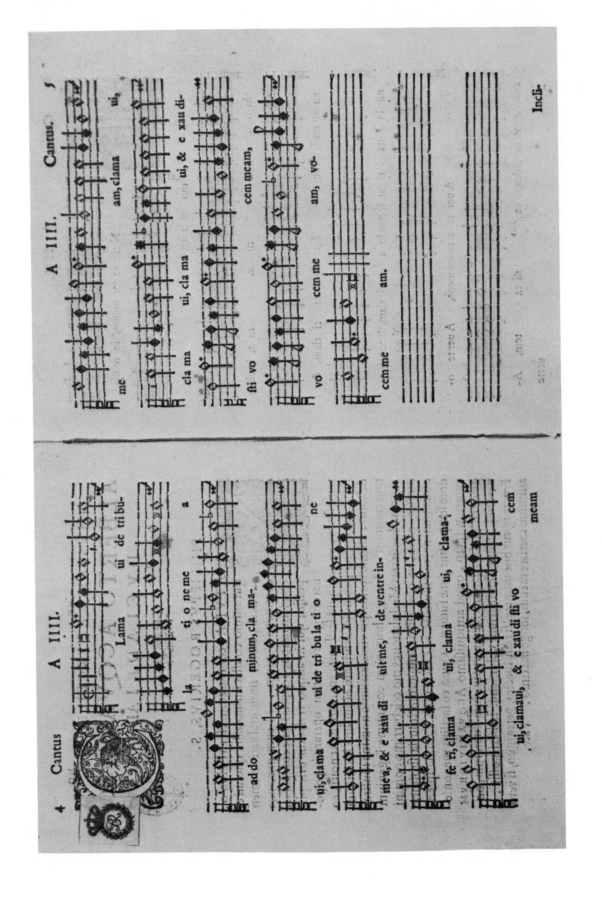

Plate II. *Cantus, Philippi Rogerii, ... sacrarum modulationum, quas vulgo Motecta appellant . . .* (1595): pages four and five

Preface

The Flemish singers whom Charles V carried about with him on his travels through Europe no doubt inspired the high regard in which his son, Philip II of Spain, held the musicians of Flanders. When Philip set up his court at Madrid in 1561 he recruited most of its musical personnel in the Low Countries, from which, over a period of nearly forty years, large numbers of choirboys traveled south to serve the royal establishment. Although Philip did maintain two chapels, one staffed by Flemish musicians and the other by Spanish, the Flemish chapel was by far the larger and finer of the two, and the Spanish singers were led by the Flemish chapelmaster. The evident favoritism of the king must have contributed to the general unpopularity which the foreigners, as representatives of a people who vexed Spain mightily during the sixteenth century, suffered in his service. The ill feeling they seem to have aroused — they were gradually purged from the court not long after Philip's death — may be accountable for the nearly total obscurity into which their music has fallen.

Philippe Rogier and his vice-chapelmaster, Géry de Ghersem, may properly be considered the last representatives of the Flemish musical tradition at the court in Madrid, a tradition that began with Pierre de Manchicourt in the early years of Philip II's reign and ended when Mateo Romero — a Fleming by birth but, it seems, a thoroughgoing Spaniard in culture — was appointed chapelmaster shortly after the death of Philip II.[1] The known details of Rogier's life are few and simple.[2] He was born about 1561 (at Arras, according to the title of a volume of his masses[3]), and began his musical career the way his predecessors as chapelmaster had begun theirs, as a choirboy. When Gérard de Turnhout was appointed chapelmaster by Philip II in 1571, the ranks of the choir needed replenishing, as was usually the case when the chapel changed hands. In the following year Turnhout traveled to the Low Countries and returned with a number of boy sopranos, among them Rogier, who arrived in Madrid on June 15, 1572.

In keeping with his usual policy toward promising choirboys, Philip II must have provided Rogier with a certain amount of education. The purpose of the king's education was to prepare his young charges for the priesthood; his general practice was to send the boys, after their voices had changed, back to the Low Countries to universities such as Douai, Tournai, or Louvain. No evidence exists to show that Rogier returned home for schooling. It can be fairly well established, however, that he was an ordained priest; in the dedication preceding the 1595 collection of his motets, the initial "S." — the usual abbreviation for *sacerdos* — is placed after his name, and in the roster of the royal chapel Rogier is listed among the chaplains beginning in 1586.

Rogier's assumption of a responsible post in the chapel coincided with the completion of the Escorial, the evolution of which must have had a considerable effect on the music composed for the court.[4] In 1584 — when Philip's masons were putting the finishing touches to the palace, monastery, and mausoleum begun twenty-one years earlier — Rogier was appointed assistant chapelmaster under George de La Hèle, chapelmaster since 1581, under whose vigorous leadership the musical establishment of the king had begun its most brilliant flowering. In 1585 Rogier traveled with the chapel to Zaragoza for the nuptial festivities of Charles Emmanuel I and the Infanta of Castile, for which he wrote a mass, *Ave martyr gloriosa* (*a* 6), and a motet, *In illo tempore accesserunt ad Jesum* (*a* 8).[5] Upon the death of de La Hèle, probably September 3, 1586, Rogier took over the direction of music at the court.

On March 2, 1590, Rogier traveled to the Low Countries to recruit four chaplains, three contrabasses, and an assistant for himself. The last Flemish choirboys to come to Spain — a dozen of them — were brought there at Rogier's behest in 1594.[6]

Although Rogier can hardly be said to have achieved great renown during his lifetime, his merits were on occasion materially recognized. As early as May, 1581, he was granted a non-residential benefice at the Church of Notre Dame in Yvoir. Before the death of the bishop of Tournai in 1592, Philip II had written asking him to award Rogier the first prebend vacant at his cathedral. After the bishop's death the request was renewed in a letter, dated February 27, 1593, to the king's cousin, Count Mansfeldt, governor general of the Low Countries;[7] whether the request was fulfilled remains to be established. In 1590 the cathedral of Toledo gave Rogier 30 ducats for a volume of his masses, sumptuously bound in calf,[8] and at the time of his death Rogier was receiving an annual pension of 300 ducats from the bishop of Léon.[9]

Rogier died on February 29, 1596, a mere 35 years old. His last work, mentioned as such in the catalog of music in the library of King John IV of Portugal, was *Toedet anima mea* (*a* 6), written for a mass of the dead.[10] In his will Rogier entrusted his student Géry de Ghersem with the publication of five of his masses, for which support had been promised by the king; the commission was discharged in 1598.

Rogier is mentioned by his famous contemporary Lope de Vega in the fourth *silva* of the *Laurel de Apolo,* written in 1630. The "shepherd Pesquera" named in the following passage, addressed to a river, is a poet whose verses Rogier set to music; Palomares is an instrumentalist and composer from Seville.

> But now the love songs
> Of your shepherd Pesquera,
> Who was love's (shepherd),
> Beg you to remember
> That he was the honor of your verdant shores,
> And the one who sang bucolic songs
> For Philippe Rogier and Palomares;
> Rogier, honor, glory, and light of Flanders,
> And Palomares of illustrious Seville;
> Both left this life in the flower of their genius,
> Depriving us of their sweet songs.[11]

A reliable assessment of Rogier's music may never be possible; his 51 known extant works — eight masses (two of which are arrangements of the same material for different forces), 36 motets, three miscellaneous sacred works, and four chansons — amount to little more than a fifth of what he is thought to have produced. In the library of King John IV of Portugal, destroyed in the Lisbon earthquake of 1755, Rogier was represented by 243 compositions, including eight masses, two magnificats, two antiphons, two responsories, 27 verses, 66 motets, 65 chansons, and 71 villancicos.[12] Other works by Rogier were no doubt housed in the library of the Spanish royal chapel, destroyed by fire in 1734.

Because the exact limits of Rogier's remaining legacy have not yet been defined, an attempt at anything so would-be-conclusive as a "style summary" of the available fraction of his output would be premature, and I have for that reason limited myself in these paragraphs to the casual discussion of certain intriguing features of the extant works. The surviving music of Rogier is interesting in a number of respects, since it exhibits both old-fashioned traits and progressive tendencies. A conservative trait of Rogier's is his interest in basing works on a cantus firmus, a procedure for which Palestrina showed little concern.[13] The *a* 5 motet *Da pacem Domine* (page 36 of the present collection) has a cantus firmus in the altus drawn from a Gregorian-chant hymn for peace. In another *Da pacem Domine* (*a* 6), in manuscript in the Escorial, the same cantus firmus appears as a canon in two tenor voices. The second superius of the motet *Salva nos, Domine* (for superius I and II and altus I and II) employs a cantus firmus based on the chant antiphon of the same name.

Rogier also shows an interest in applying paraphrase technique to melodic lines. In *Da pacem Domine* (*a* 5 the head — the first few notes — of the chant melody is reproduced in voices other than the cantus firmus; after each appearance of the head of the chant, the remainder of the line is allowed to develop in an improvisatory manner. In the motet *Regina caeli* (page 106 of this edition), paraphrase technique is especially apparent, in that the melodic lines are clearly related to the Gregorian-chant antiphon.

Various contrapuntal devices characteristic of an era earlier than his own appear frequently in Rogier's music. An example is provided by the motet *Sancta Maria* (page 58 of this edition), which has a voice in canon with the quintus; interestingly, Rogier gives neither *resolutio* for the canon nor directions as to the interval at which the canon is to be sung, only an indication of the point at which the canonic voice must enter. An outstanding repository of archaic contrapuntal devices in Rogier's work is the 159- mass *Philippus Secundus, Rex Hispaniae* (*a* 4), based on a *soggetto cavato* of eleven notes which appears throughout the tenor.

Among the progressive tendencies that may be observed in Rogier's compositions is the persistent appearance in some of the motets, especially those for six and more voices, of short note values. The two motets beginning with the words *Cantate Domino* (pages 86 and 93 of this collection) and the eight-voice double-chorus motet *Regina caeli* show an abundance of fusas and semifusas. The treatment of the text in these motets is frequently not in ccord with standard sixteenth-century practice; very often usas are made to carry separate syllables.

Rogier's musical texture may also be considered progresive. Of his eight extant masses three are for more than ne chorus, and one of these is for three choruses; of his notets one is for two choruses and another is for three. A continuo part for organ is often included in these works, nd in the three-chorus motet *Verbum caro* the harp is he continuo instrument accompanying one of the choruses. Leichtentritt cites this motet as providing a late-sixteenth century example of the use of an independent continuo line, a practice which, of course, became nearly universal in he seventeenth century.[14]

Still another advanced practice of Rogier's can be observed in the works with continuo, which also include a eparate part for the director of the ensemble. The part is narked *guion* (leader), and consists of the lowest line ormed by the bass parts of the piece taken together.

During the sixteenth century the dukes of Atri, although riginally from the Abruzzi, maintained a residential palace n Naples, a Spanish possession at the time. The dukes of Atri were of the Acquaviva family, which, during the sixeenth and seventeenth centuries, supplied an imposing number of persons to the hierarchy of the Roman Catholic hurch, among them Giulio Acquaviva, Pius V's nuncio to he court of Philip II. The closeness of the relationship etween the family of Acquaviva and the court of Spain luring the late sixteenth century is attested in some small neasure by Rogier's dedication of his 1595 motets to Albert Acquaviva, Duke of Atri, and by the publication f the work in Naples. It is from a copy of that collection elonging to the Biblioteca Nacional in Madrid, Spain, hat the eleven motets in this edition are taken.

The title page of the cantus part-book of the motets eads: "CANTUS,/PHILIPPI ROGERII,/INVICTISS.ᵐⁱ PHILIPPI II./ HISPANIARUM REGIS, ETC./CHORI MUSICI PRÆFECTI./SACRARUM MODULATIONUM, QUAS VULGO/Motecta appellant: quæ Quaernis, Quinis, Senis, &/octonis vocibus concinuntur./LIBER PRIMUS./NEAPOLI, Ex Typogr. Stelliolæ, ad Portam Regalem." The music (fully inventoried on page 13, elow) is in six part-books printed with movable type imilar to that used by Pierre Phalèse at Antwerp, but vith gracefully ornamented initial letters from a font more characteristically Italian than Flemish. The imprint "Ex

Typographia Stelliolæ, ad Portam Regalem. MDXCV." appears at the end of each part-book, with the imprimatur of Ardicinus Biandrà, Vicar General of Naples.

The present edition is limited by the available space to a selection of eleven of the sixteen motets in the original collection. I made my choice on the basis of musical interest, although the motets left out of the edition are by no means uninteresting.

The texts of some of the motets suit them to performance in a wide range of circumstances; the texts of others make them necessarily quite occasional. The following list shows the sources of the texts and their use in the Roman Catholic liturgy:[15]

Clamavi: similar to Psalm 119, 1. Used on Monday at vespers, *Liber Usualis*, 281.

Inclina cor meum: Psalm 118, 36-7. Used on Sunday at terce, *Liber Usualis*, 236. Short responsory in *Liber Usualis*, 237-8.

Dominus regit me and its *secunda pars*, *Super aquam*: Psalm 22, 1-3. Used in the office of the dead at matins, second nocturn, *Liber Usualis*, 1788.

Da pacem Domine: an old antiphon for peace, from the *Antiphonale Romano* of the time of St. Gregory I (590-604). Both the text and the melody which Rogier uses as a cantus firmus may be found in *Liber Usualis*, 1867-8.

Vias tuas and its *secunda pars*, *Delicta iuventutis meae*: Psalm 24, 4-5 and 7-8. Used in the office of the dead at matins, second nocturn, *Liber Usualis*, 1788-9.

Sancta Maria: an antiphon for first vespers of the common office of the Blessed Virgin Mary, *Liber Usualis*, 1254-5.

Cantantibus organis: appears in a slightly different version as the first antiphon in second vespers for the feast of St. Cecilia, November 22, *Liber Usualis*, 1756.

Laboravi: Psalm 6, 7 (verse 6 of the Psalm as it appears in *Liber Usualis*). Used on Monday at compline, *Liber Usualis*, 283, and in the office of the dead at matins, first nocturn, *Liber Usualis*, 1783.

Cantate Domino canticum novum, cantate Domino omnis terra: Psalm 95, 1-3. Used at matins for the feast of Christmas, *Liber Usualis*, 387.

Cantate Domino canticum novum, quia mirabilia fecit and its *secunda pars*, *Recordatus est*: Psalm 97, 1-3. Used at matins for the feast of Christmas, *Liber Usualis*, 388.

Regina caeli: an antiphon in honor of the Virgin Mary

used on Sunday at compline during the Easter season. Both the text and the melody that Rogier paraphrased may be found in the *Liber Usualis, 275.*

In the present edition the note values of the source have been reduced by one half. Original clefs and the original position and value of the first note in each voice are shown at the beginning of each motet. In accordance with usual sixteenth-century practice the final note of each voice in the source is a longa, transcribed in this edition as a whole note with a hold placed over it, occupying a complete measure.

Ligatures are indicated by horizontal brackets: ♩ ♩ , for example, indicates a ligature of two semibreves in the original. Coloration in a ligature is shown by a dashed line placed above the blackened note: ♩ ♩. ♪ .

All accidentals and cancellations save those in brackets or parentheses are Rogier's, including, of course, all the signs present in the source except those made redundant by the bar-lines I have supplied. With the intention of making sight-reading of the scores easier for performers, I have bracketed editorial accidentals and put them before, rather than above, their notes. Both original and editorial accidentals apply to all repetitions of the same pitch within a measure, unless deliberately cancelled. I have used cancellations in parentheses both (a) to clarify the duration of original accidentals, and (b) to cancel editorial accidentals.

I have applied *musica ficta* conservatively, but I have not hesitated to use it where it is obviously required. My most common reasons for its use are the melodic correction of augmented fourths and diminished fifths to perfect intervals, the assurance of perfect octaves harmonically, and the raising of the leading tone at interior cadences, but I have often decided to add or not to add an editorial accidental on the basis of general melodic, harmonic, and textual considerations. The users of this edition are, of course, at liberty to dispute any of my decisions.

Except in certain mechanical particulars, the texts of the edition follow the source faithfully. I have brought spelling and word-division into accord with current ecclesiastical usage. Punctuation is original except where I have done away with inconsistencies among voices or sections of a piece. Straight lines have been used where necessary to extend undivided words or the final syllables of words under more than one note. Text is carefully underlaid in the original collection, and text placements in this edition which seem to violate sixteenth-century standards follow the clear indications of the source. Passages whose repetition is indicated in the source by the abbreviation *ij* have been underlaid and placed in brackets. In a few cases of exceptionally awkward text underlay, I have made changes, as follows:

Page 57, measure 71, tenor: "tu" moved from beat 2 to beat 1.

Page 108, measure 24, chorus II, bassus: "le" moved from C to A.

Page 109, measure 36, chorus I, altus: "le" moved from G beat 2 to G second half of beat 3.

In the following instances I have corrected clear errors of notation in the source or removed signs that are apparently superfluous:

Page 28, measure 80, cantus, beat 2: natural sign deleted.

Page 40, measure 62, quintus, beat 2: A minim changed to A semibreve.

Page 57, measure 74, quintus, beat 3: E semibreve changed to D semibreve.

Page 66, measure 97, altus: sharp sign removed from the final G longa.

Page 80, measure 39, sextus, beat 4: natural sign deleted.

Page 93, measure 5, sextus, second quarter of beat 2: G semifusa changed to F semifusa.

Page 96, measure 38, tenor, beat 3: C semibreve changed to D semibreve.

Page 97, measure 44, altus, beat 3: A semibreve changed to G semibreve.

Page 99, measure 57, quintus, beat 2: natural sign deleted.

Page 105, measure 61, bassus: G semibreve in ligature changed to G longa.

Page 109, measure 35, chorus II, cantus, second quarter of beat 2: F fusa changed to G fusa.

Page 109, measure 37, chorus II, cantus, second quarter of beat 2: F fusa changed to A fusa.

I am grateful to the Biblioteca Nacional in Madrid, Spain, for allowing me to use the materials on which this edition is based.

Lavern J. Wagner
Quincy College
Quincy, Illinois

June, 1966

The Works of Philippe Rogier

A total of 243 works by Rogier, listed in the catalog of the library of King John IV of Portugal,° were lost when the library was destroyed by the Lisbon earthquake of 1755. The burning of the Spanish royal chapel in 1734 also caused the destruction of a great quantity of music written by the Netherlanders active in Spain during the sixteenth century. The following list incorporates all of Rogier's surviving works that have been located to date.

Masses

I. *Missae Sex/Philippi Rogerii/Atrebatensis sacelli/Regi Phonasci Musicae/peritissimi, & aetatis suae facile/Principis./Ad Philippum Tertium/Hispaniarum Regem./Matriti/ex typographia Regia,/MDXCVIII*, in 257 pages folio. The publication includes five masses by Rogier — *Philippus Secundus, Rex Hispaniae* (*a* 4), *Inclita stirps Jesse* (*a* 4), *Dirige gressus meos* (*a* 5), *Ego sum qui sum* (*a* 6), *Inclina Domine* (*a* 6) — and one by Rogier's pupil Géry de Ghersem, *Ave Virgo sanctissima* (*a* 7). Copies of the collection survive in Germany: Neuberg/Donau, Staatliche Bibliothek (Provinzialbibliothek); in Spain: Córdoba, Archivo de la Catedral, Madrid, Biblioteca Nacional (lacking pp. 249-257), Málaga, Archivo de la Catedral, Toledo, Archivo de la Catedral, and Valladolid, Archivo de la Catedral; in Portugal: Coimbra, Biblioteca Geral da Universidade; in Peru: Cuzco Cathedral; and in Mexico: Puebla Cathedral. A copy in the library at Tournai was destroyed during World War II. Manuscript scores of the five masses by Rogier are at the Real Colegio de Corpus Christi (Patriarca) in Valencia, Spain. The mass *Inclita stirps Jesse* from this collection was reprinted by Robert van Maldeghem in *Trésor Musicale, Musique Religieuse* (1885), XXI, 3.

II. Mass *Domine Dominus Noster*. Two versions survive, one *a* 8 for two choruses with continuos for two organs, and one *a* 12 for three choruses with continuos for three organs. Both are in manuscript at the Escorial; a manuscript of the version for three choruses is also at the Real Colegio de Corpus Christi (Patriarca) in Valencia, and a manuscript of the continuo to this version is at the Cathedral in Palma, Mallorca. The popularity of this mass is attested by two reductions at the Cathedral in Valladolid, "Redución de una misa de Rogier a 12 voces a 5" by an anonymous author, and "Sobre la misa de Philippe Rogier" by Camargo.

III. Mass *Domine in Virtute tua* (*a* 8). The manuscript is at the Cathedral in Valladolid.

Motets and Miscellaneous Sacred Works

I. *Cantus,/Philippi Rogerii,/invictiss.ᵐⁱ Philippi II./Hispaniarum Regis, etc./chori musici praefecti./sacrarum modulationum, quas vulgo/Motecta appellant: quae Quaternis, Quinis, Senis &/octonis vocibus concinuntur./liber primus./Neapoli, Ex Typogr. Stelliolae, ad Portam Regalem*, in part-books: cantus, 42 pages; sextus, 31 pages; altus, 42 pages; quintus, 39 pages; tenor, 42 pages; bassus, 40 pages. The publication includes the following motets, of which those reproduced in this edition are marked with an asterisk: °*Clamavi* (*a* 4), °*Inclina cor meum* (*a* 4), °*Dominus regit me* and its *secunda pars*, °*Super aquam* (both *a* 5), °*Da pacem Domine* (*a* 5), *Paries quidem filium* (*a* 5), *Locutus sum in lingua mea* and its *secunda pars, Veruntamen* (both *a* 6), °*Vias tuas* and its *secunda pars*, °*Delicta iuventutis meae* (both *a* 6), °*Sancta Maria* (*a* 6), *Caligaverunt oculi mei* and its *secunda pars, Qui consolabatur me* (both *a* 6), *Sit gloria Domini* (*a* 6), °*Cantantibus organis* (*a* 6), °*Laboravi* (*a* 6), *Peccavi* and its *secunda pars, Ecce nunc* (both *a* 6), °*Cantate Domino . . . omnis terra* (*a* 6), °*Cantate Domino . . . quia mirabilia fecit* and its *secunda pars*, °*Recordatus est* (both *a* 6), and °*Regina caeli* (*a* 8, for two choruses). Copies of the collection are at Madrid, Biblioteca Nacional; Valladolid, Archivo de la Catedral; and Segovia, Archivo Capitular de la Catedral (altus, quintus, and tenor part books only). The motet *Regina caeli* survives separately at the Cathedral in Valladolid. A freely-modified version of this motet is at the Cathedral in Valencia, and a copy from which pages are missing is at the Real Colegio de Corpus Christi (Patriarca) in Valencia.

° Joaquim de Vasconcelos, ed., *Primeira Parte do Indexa Da Livraria de Musico do Muyto Alto e Poderoso Rey Dom Ioão o IV. Nosso Senhor, Por ordem de Sua Mag. por Paulo Craesbeck, Anno 1649.* Compiled for the royal library in Lisbon; reprinted at Porto in 1874. These works are also listed by Edmond Vander Straeten in *La Musique aux Pays-Bas avant le XIXᵉ siècle* (Bruxelles, 1867-88), VIII, 505-10.

II. Motets in manuscript at the Escorial include *Justus es Domine* (*a* 5), *Cantate Domino* (*a* 5), *Respice in me* (*a* 5), *Venit lumen tuum* (*a* 5), *Justus es Domine* (*a* 5 — a second setting, for lower voices only), *Descendit angelus* (*a* 5), *Verba mea auribus* (*a* 5), *Heu mihi Domine* (*a* 5), *Pereat dies* (*a* 5), *Da pacem Domine* (*a* 6), and *Verbum caro* (*a* 12, for three choruses).

III. Motet *Salva nos, Domine* (*a* 4, for treble voices). Two manuscript copies of this work are owned by the Hispanic Society of America, New York. The original title page of each is missing; folio 2 has the title *Siguense las 16. magnificas de morales.*

IV. Motet *Laudate Dominum in Sanctis eius* (*a* 8). Manuscripts of this work are at the Cathedral and the Real Colegio de Corpus Christi (Patriarca) in Valencia.

V. *Cinco lecciones* from the office of the dead are in manuscript at the Cathedral in Valladolid: *Tedet animam meam, Domine si fuise, Credo quod redemptor meus, Modicum et non videbitis,* and *Erat Jesu eiiciens* (all *a* 5). A *Tedet animam meam* (*a* 6) is in score at the Real Colegio de Corpus Christi (Patriarca) in Valencia.

VI. Motet *Videntes stellam* (*a* 12) is in manuscript at the Cathedral in Segovia, with a *Responsorio de la Natividad* (*a* 12), *Incarnatus est* (Solo), and an "Acompañamiento organo" (*a* 12).

Chansons

I. *Le Rossignol musical des chansons de diverses et excellens autheurs de nostre temps a quatre, cinq et six parties. Novellement recueillé & mises in lumière,* Antwerpen, P. Phalèse, 1597, reprinted 1598, in five part books, 4° obl. Four chansons by Rogier are in this collection: *Tout le plaisir* (*a* 5), *Amour et la beauté* (*a* 5), *Veu que de vostr'amour* (*a* 6), and *Leal amour* (*a* 6). Copies of the collection survive in Poland: Danzig, Biblioteka Polskiej Akademii Nauk (1597 edition); in Sweden: Uppsala, Universitetsbibioteket (1597 edition, tenor only); in Belgium: Brussels, Bibliothèque Royale de Belgique (1598 edition, quintus

lacking); and in Great Britain: London, Westminster Abbey (1598 edition, quintus only).

II. The following chansons, supposed by various scholars to have been composed by Philippe Rogier, are attributed in their sources simply to "Rogier"; the assumption that "Rogier" is Philip II's chapelmaster is hazardous, since at least one other composer — Rogier-Pathie — could have been intended by the attribution. (a) *Noble fleur* and *Sans mot, sans nulz mot* (both *a* 4, bassus lacking) are in manuscript at the Biblioteca del Conservatorio in Florence, Italy; they are attributed to Philippe Rogier by J. B. Trend in *Grove's Dictionary of Music and Musicians* (New York, 1954), VII, 205, and by Florimond van Duyse in *Biographie Nationale de Belgique* (Bruxelles, 1866-1944), XIX, 813. (b) *Du moy de may* (originally for four voices) appears in lute transcription in *Novae tabulae musicae testitudinariae hexachordae et heptachordae. Julij Caesaris Barbetti Paduani,* Strasbourg, B. Jobin, 1582, of which copies survive in Germany: Donaueschingen, Fürstl. Fürstenbergische Hofbibliothek; in Poland: Wroclaw, Biblioteka Uniwersytecka; and in the United States: Washington, D.C., Library of Congress. The work is attributed to "P. Rogier" in *Répertoire International des Sources Musicales. Recueils imprimés XVIᵉ-XVIIᵉ siècles* (München, 1960-), I, 315. (c) *Doulce memoire* (*a* 4) appears in *La Bataglia Francese et Canzon delli Ucelli Insieme alcune Canzoni Francese, Partite in Caselle per sonar d'instromento perfetto: Novamente Ristampate,* Venetia, Gardano, 1577, of which a copy belongs to the Museo Civico di Bibliografia Musicale in Bologna, Italy. The work is attributed to Philippe Rogier by Ferdinand Haberl in *Die Musik in Geschichte und Gegenwart* (Kassel, 1949-), XI, 638. *Ce n'est pas tout,* published by Robert van Maldeghem in *Trésor Musicale, Musique Profane* (1883), XIX, 12, is by Rogier Pathie (Maître Rogier). In *Trésor Musicale, Musique Religieuse* (1885), XXI, index, Rogier-Pathie is confused with Philippe Rogier, the author of the mass *Inclita stirp Jesse* in that volume.

Notes

[1]Although it was long supposed by many that Mateo Romero was a native Spaniard (as argued in Higinio Anglés and Joaquin Pena, *Diccionario de la Música Labor* (Barcelona, Madrid, etc., 1954), II, 1908, and Rafael Mitjana, "Commentarios y Apostillas 'Cancionero poético y musical del siglo XVII'," *Revista de Filologia Española,* VI (July-September, 1919), 241-8), it has now been definitely established that he was born at Liège. Supporting documents are reproduced in Paul Becquart, "Matheo Romero u Matthieu Rosmarin (1575-1647)," *Archives, Bibliothèques et Musèes de Belgique,* XXXIV, nos. 1-2 (1963), 11-47.

[2]In addition to the standard references — Eitner, Fétis, *Grove's,* and *Die Musik in Geschichte und Gegenwart* — the following works supply useful information about Flemish musicians in Spain generally and about Rogier specifically: Higinio Anglés and Joaquin Pena, *Diccionario de la Música Labor* (Barcelona, Madrid, etc., 1954), II, 1901-2; Paul Becquart, "Musiciens neérlandais en Espagne (fin XVIe-debut XVIIe siècle)," *Revue Belge de Musicologie,* XIV (1960), 72-80; Paul Becquart, "Quatre documents espagnols inédits relatifs à Philippe Rogier," *Revue Belge de Musicologie,* XIV (1960), 126-31; *Biographie Nationale de Belgique* (Bruxelles, 1866-1944), XIX, 812-13; Charles van den Borren, *La musique en Belgique du Moyen Age à nos jours* (Bruxelles, 1950), 133; Edmond Vander Straeten, *La Musique aux Pays-Bas avant le XIXe siècle* (Bruxelles, 1867-88), II, 12-17, III, 214-18, VIII, 111, 114, 152-236, 401, 402, 505-10, 549; Lavern J. Wagner, "Flemish Musicians at the Spanish Court of Philip II," *Caecilia,* LXXXVI, no. 3 (autumn 1959), 107-14; and Lavern J. Wagner, "The Life and Times of Flemish Boy Choristers in 16th Century Spain," *Caecilia,* XCI, no. 2 (summer 1964), 35-47.

[3]*Missae Sex/Philippi Rogerii/Atrebatensis sacelli/Regi Phonasci Musicae/peritissimi, &aetatis suae facile/Principis./Ad Philippum Tertium/Hispaniarum Regem./Matriti/ex typographia Regia,/MDXCVIII.*

[4]Rogier's works for three choirs and three organs, to take a late example, were written in the early 1590's, just after the completion of the palace organs by Gilles Brebos, himself a Fleming, in about 1590.

[5]Edmond Vander Straeten, *La Musique aux Pays-Bas avant le XIXe siècle* (Bruxelles, 1867-88), VIII, 505, 506. A contemporary account of this trip: *Relacion del viaje hecho por Felipe II, en 1585, a Zaragoza, Barcelona y Valencia, escrita por Henrique Cock* (Madrid, 1876). Cf. Vander Straeten, *op. cit.,* VIII, 112-14.

[6]Vander Straeten, *op. cit.,* VIII, 167-74. Vander Straeten provides an interesting account of the procurement of Flemish choirboys and their journey to Spain. See also Lavern J. Wagner, "The Life and Times of Flemish Boy Choristers in 16th Century Spain," *Caecilia,* XCI, no. 2 (summer 1964), 35-47.

[7]Vander Straeten, *op. cit.,* III, 217-18.

[8]*Ibid.,* VIII, 213.

[9]Paul Becquart, "Quatre documents espagnols inédits relatifs à Philippe Rogier," *Revue Belge de Musicologie,* XIV (1960), 129.

[10]Vander Straeten, *op. cit.,* VIII, 508.

[11]Pero ya las canciones amorosas
  de tu pastor Pesquera,
  que del amor lo era,
  te piden que te acuerdes
  que fué el honor de tus riberas verdes,
  y el que daba bucólicos cantares
  a Phelipe Roger y a Palomares;
  Roger, honor de Flándes, gloria y lustre,
  y Palomares de Sevilla ilustre;
  entrambos en la flor de sus deseos,
  para lograrse mal dulces Orfeos.

From *Collecion de las obras sueltas, assi en prosa, como en verso, de D. Frey Lope Felix de Vega Carpio, del habito de San Juan* (Madrid, 1776-9), I, 73-4. The passage is given by Vander Straeten, *op. cit.,* VIII, 193, but there are errors and omissions in his text.

[12]Joaquim de Vasconcelos, ed., *Primeira Parte do Indexa Da Livraria de Musico do Muyto Alto e Poderoso Rey Dom Ioão o IV. Nosso Senhor, Por ordem de Sua Mag. por Paulo Craesbeck, Anno 1649.* Compiled for the royal library in Lisbon; reprinted at Porto in 1874.

[13]H. K. Andrews, *An Introduction to the Technique of Palestrina* (London, 1958), 155, 191n.

[14]Hugo Leichtentritt, *Geschichte der Motette* (Leipzig, 1908), 375.

[15]The numbering of the Psalms mentioned is according to the Douay version of the Bible.

15

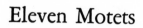

Eleven Motets

Clamavi

me - - am, vo - - cem me - - am.

sti vo - - -cem me - - am.

et e - xau - di - sti vo - - - cem me - am.

cem me - am, vo - cem me - - am.

Inclina cor meum

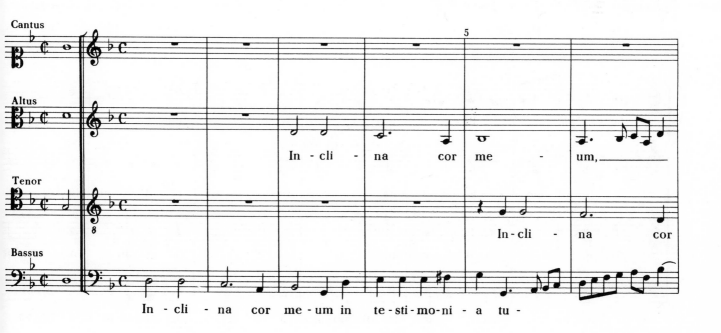

Cantus

Altus

In - cli - na cor me - um,_____

Tenor

In - cli - na cor

Bassus

In - cli - na cor me - um in te - sti - mo - ni - a tu -

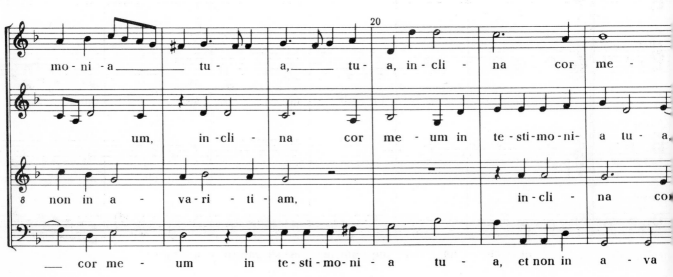

28

Dominus regit me

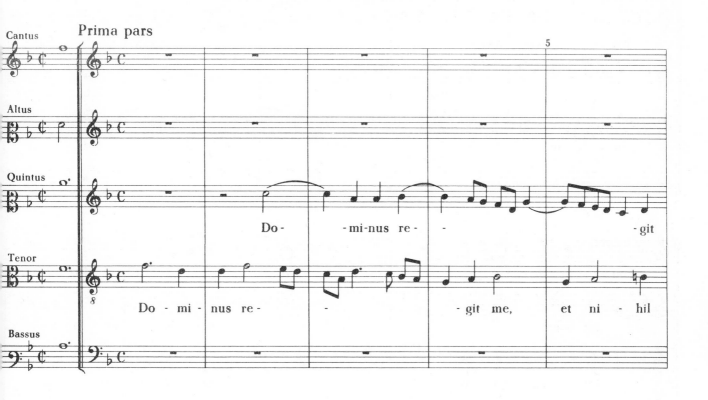

me col - lo - ca - vit, i - bi me col - lo - ca - vit.

me col - lo - ca - vit, col - lo - ca - vit.

bi me col - lo - ca - vit, col - lo - ca - vit.

lo - ca - vit, i - bi me col - lo - ca - vit.

ca - vit, i - bi me col - lo - ca - vit.

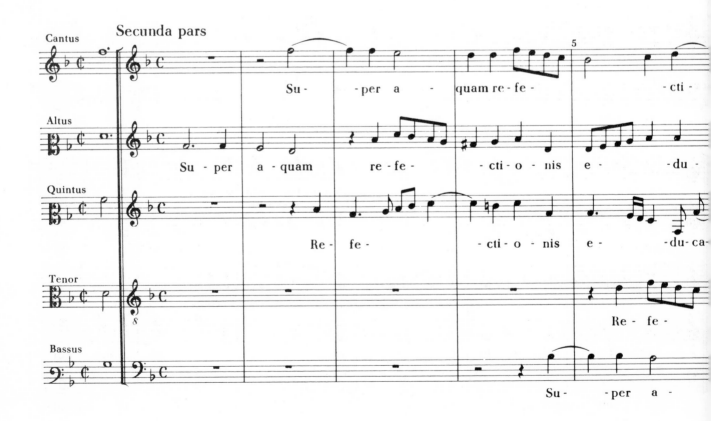

Secunda pars

Cantus

Su - per a - quam re - fe - cti

Altus

Su - per a - quam re - fe - cti - o - nis e - du

Quintus

Re - fe - cti - o - nis e - du - ca

Tenor

Re - fe

Bassus

Su - per a -

Da pacem Domine

Vias tuas

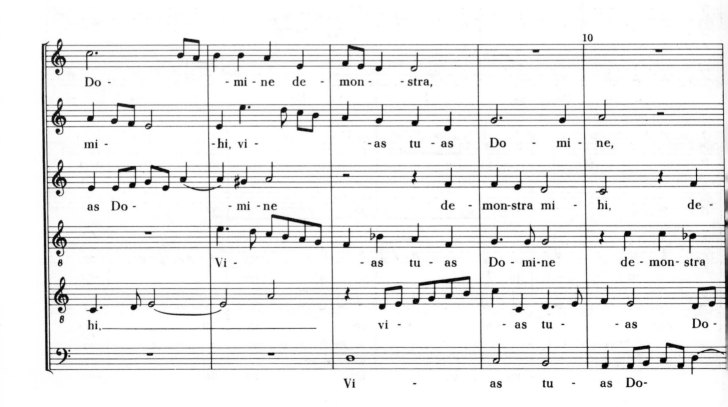

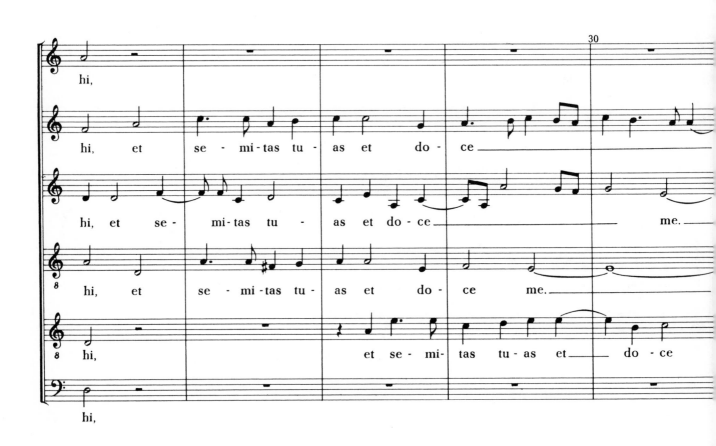

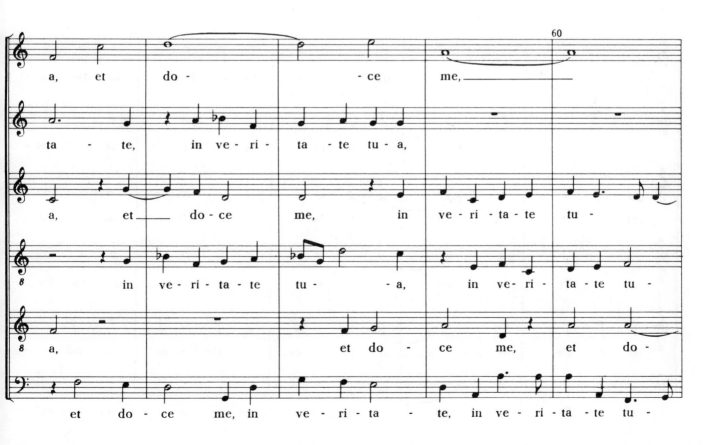

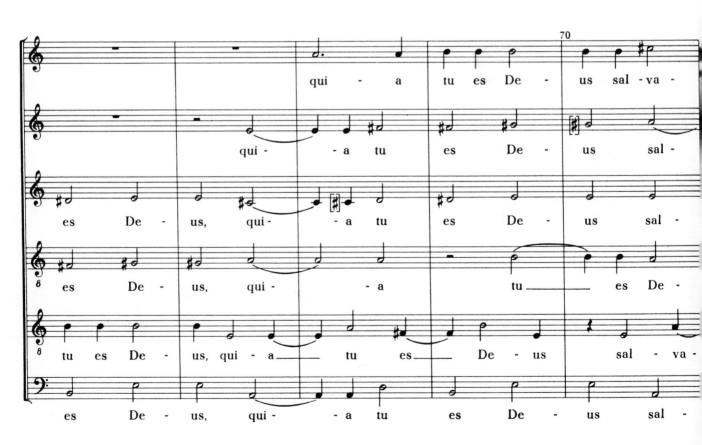

50

Secunda pars

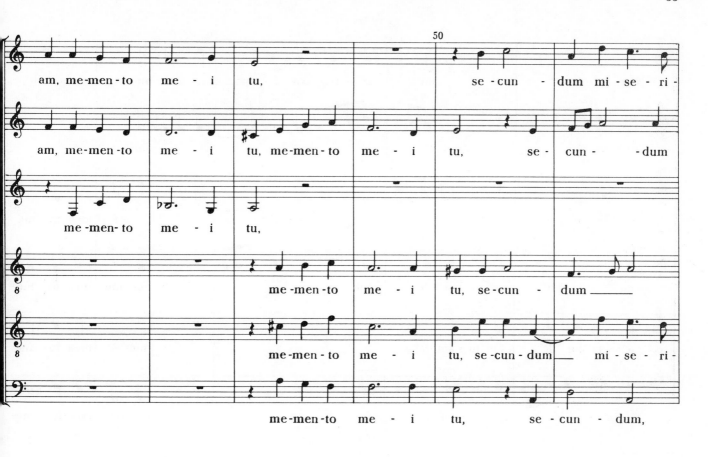

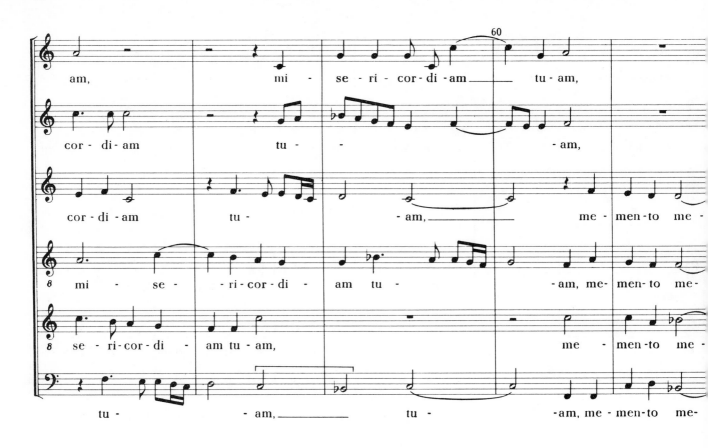

Sancta Maria

66

Cantantibus organis

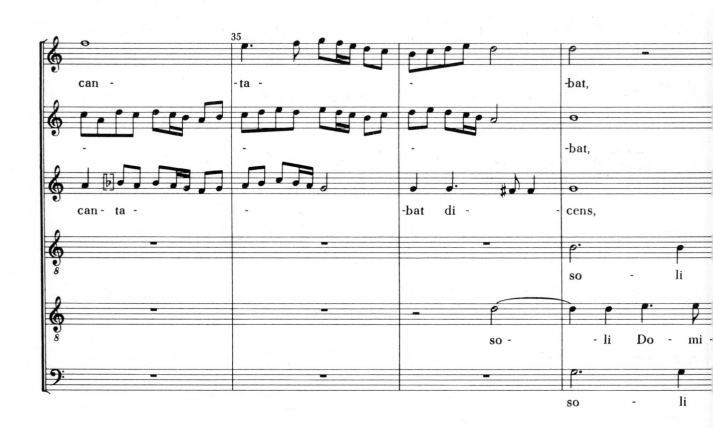

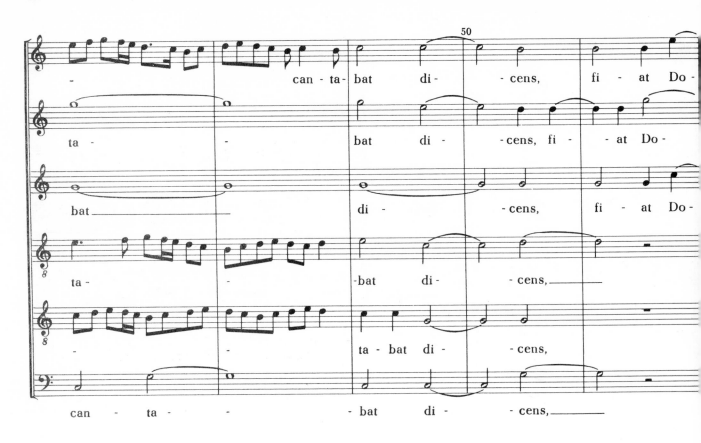

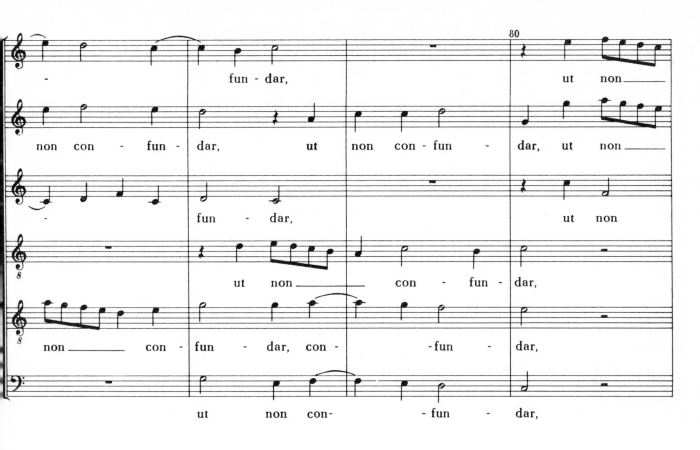

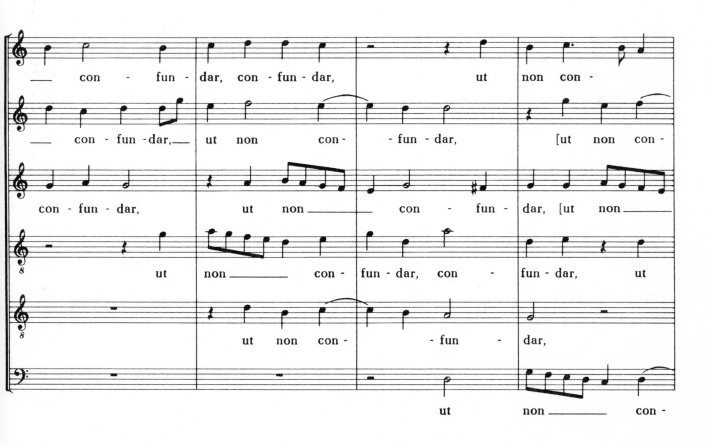

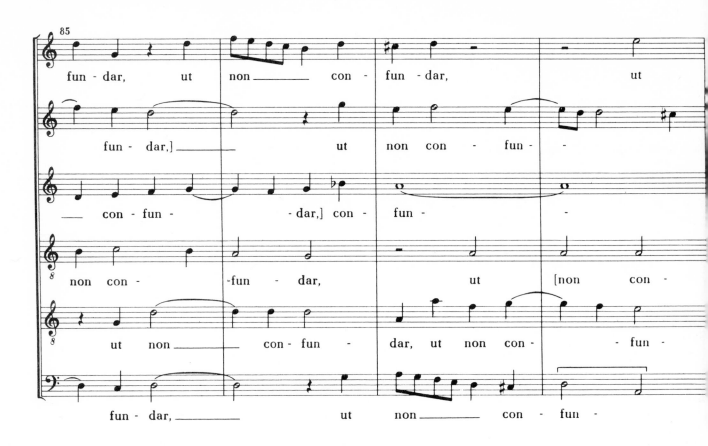

Laboravi

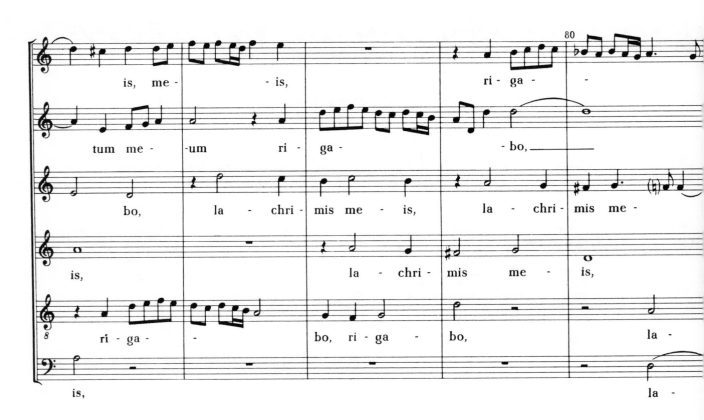

Cantate Domino canticum novum

Cantate Domino, omnis terra

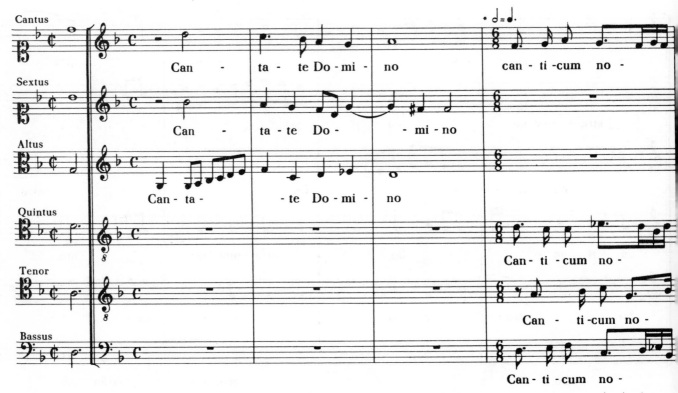

* *Original meter signature is* ₵. *Notation in original has white noteheads at this point, e.g.,* 𝅗𝅥. 𝅘𝅥𝅮 𝅘𝅥 𝅗𝅥. 𝅘𝅥𝅮 𝅘𝅥𝅮 𝅘𝅥𝅮

88

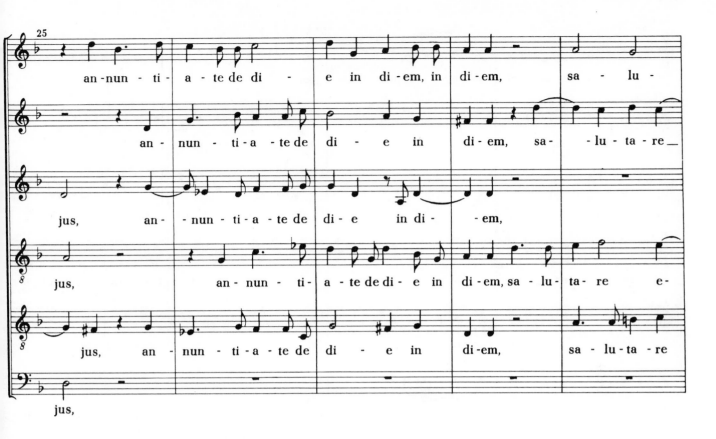

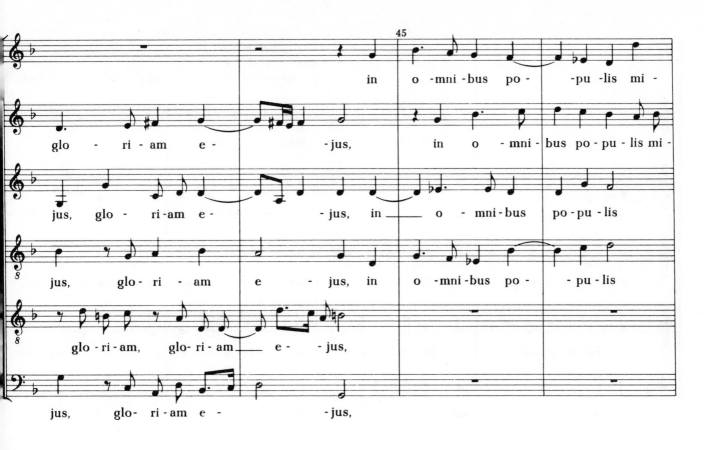

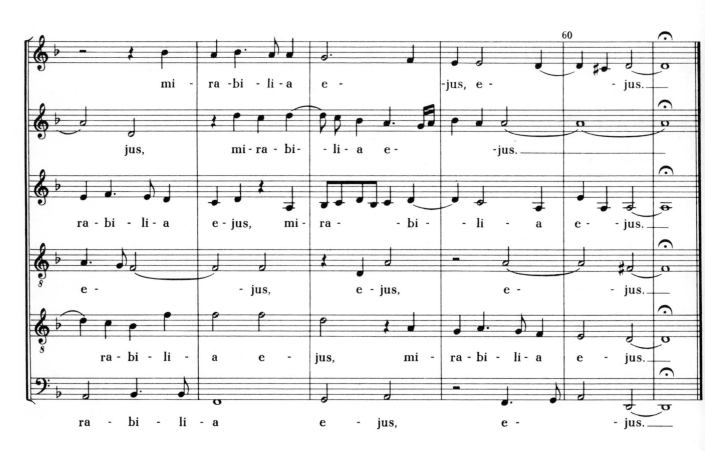

Cantate Domino canticum novum

Quia mirabilia fecit

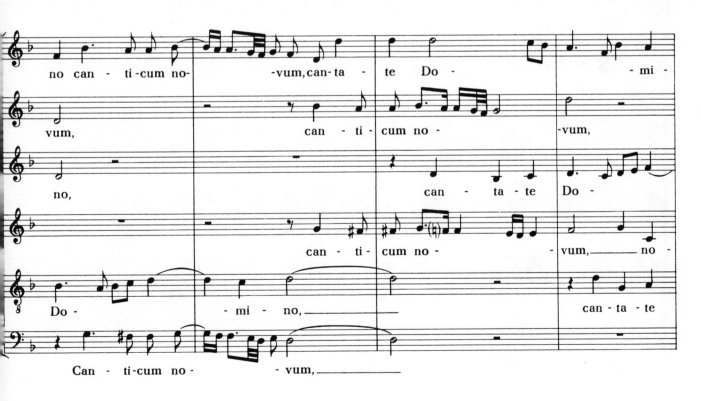

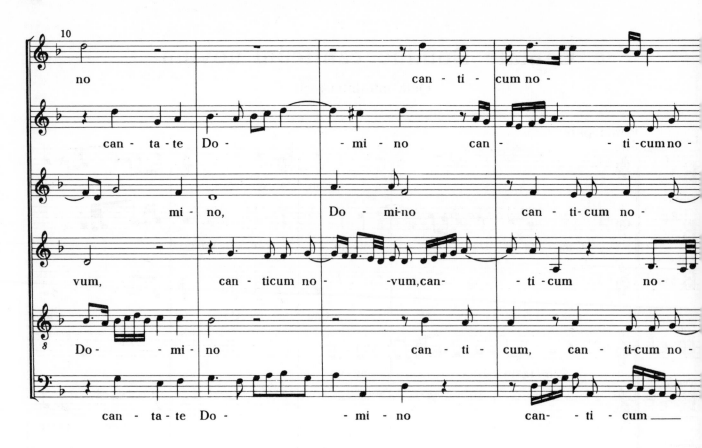

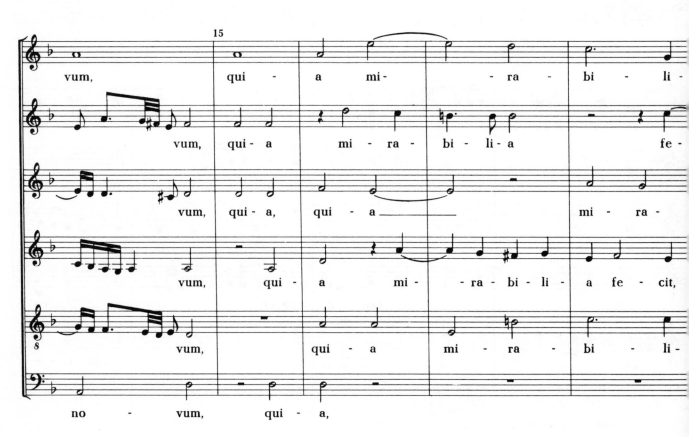

Secunda pars

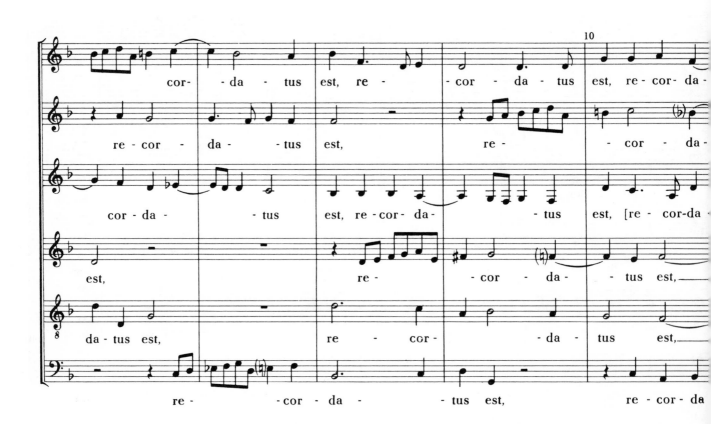

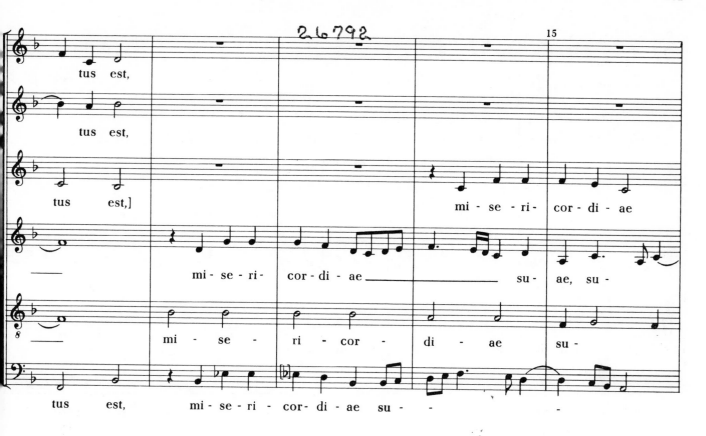

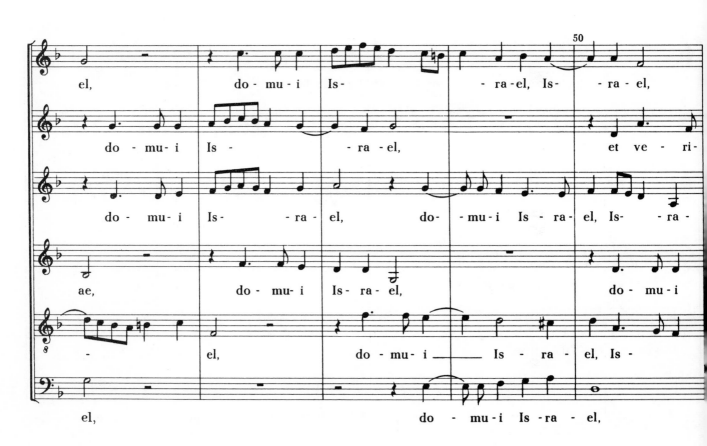

Regina caeli

* *Original meter signature is ₵ 3*